Rubbish

Claire Llewellyn

(E)

628.44

SIMON & SCHUSTER

LONDON • SYDNEY • NEW YORK • TOKYO • SINGAPORE • TORONTO

S327657

Notes for parents and teachers

This book has a theme that threads its way through the subject of the book. It does not aim to deal with the topic comprehensively; rather it aims to provoke thought and discussion. Each page heading makes a simple statement about the illustration which is then amplified and questioned by the text. Material in this book is particularly relevant to the following sections of the National Curriculum for England and Wales:

English: AT1 levels 1–2, AT2 levels 1–3
Science: AT5 levels 1–5

In Scotland the proposals of the Scottish Education Department apply.

TAKE ONE has been researched and compiled by Simon & Schuster Young Books. We are very grateful for the support and guidance provided by our advisory panel of professional educationalists in the course of the production.

Advisory panel:
Colin Pidgeon, Headteacher
Wheatfields Junior School, St Albans
Deirdre Walker, Deputy headteacher
Wheatfields Junior School, St Albans
Judith Clarke, Headteacher
Grove Infants School, Harpenden

Series editor: Daphne Butler
Design: M&M Design Partnership
Photographs: Ecoscene pages 7, 11, 12 (top), 15, 18, 19, 20, 23, 26, 28 (top left and bottom); ZEFA cover and pages 8, 10, 12 (bottom), 16, 25, 27; Nigel Dennis/NHPA page 21 and Stephen Dalton/NHPA page 24; Heather Angel page 28 (top right)

First published in Great Britain in 1991 by Simon & Schuster Young Books

Simon & Schuster Young Books
Simon & Schuster Ltd
Wolsey House, Wolsey Road
Hemel Hempstead, Herts HP2 4SS

British Library Cataloguing in Publication Data
Llewellyn, Claire
  Rubbish
  1. Waste materials. Processing
  I. Title II. Series
  628.445

ISBN 0–7500–0926–8

Printed and bound in Great Britain by BPCC Hazell Books, Paulton and Aylesbury

Contents

Everybody has rubbish

Every person in every house in every
town or village generates rubbish.

What kinds of things do we call rubbish?
Many of them are in the picture.
Can you think of any that aren't?

Where does most of our rubbish come from?

26398-Y
N.Y. OFFICIAL 'IV

25N·111

CAUTION

8

Collecting the rubbish

We put most of our rubbish in a
dustbin.   Each week, dustmen and women
visit every street, empty the rubbish
into a dustcart and take it away.

It is a dirty but important job.

What would happen if they
stopped coming?

Rubbish disposal

There are different ways of disposing of rubbish.   In many places, it is taken to a special site outside the town and covered over with earth.

In other places the rubbish is emptied into a huge oven and burned.

Do you know what happens to the rubbish in your town?

11

12

That's not rubbish!

Not all of our rubbish needs to be thrown away.   Some of it can be used again – like the empty milk bottles people put on the doorstep each day.

Some of our rubbish can't be used again, but it can help to make new materials. This is called recycling.

Do you know any materials that can be recycled?

New metal from old cans

People take their empty cans to a
special bin called the can bank.

The old cans are fed into a machine
which squashes them into square bales.
The bales are taken to a metal factory
and turned into sheets of metal.

The metal from steel cans is used in
building.   The metal from aluminium
cans is used to make new cans.

15

Recycling saves waste

Using old materials to make new goods means we don't have to use new materials.   We can save them.

We make paper from trees.   If we recycle used paper – for boxes, books and paper bags – trees will be saved.

More goods are now made from recycled materials.   They carry this symbol ♻ .

Nature makes rubbish, too

Nature may not make waste paper or empty cans, but it has plenty of rubbish to dispose of.

What happens to the leaves that fall from the trees in autumn?   Are they still there in the spring?

18

Nature's dustmen

We rarely find the bodies of dead animals and birds.   Yet there are millions of them in the world.   What happens to their bodies when they die?

Which insects, animals and birds clear up animal remains?

The litter problem

When rubbish is left lying around we call it litter.

Litter is unsightly.   It spoils the look of a place – in the town or the country.

How does the litter get there? What happens to it?

23

Litter can be harmful

Metal cans and broken glass bottles
have sharp edges.   Where is this kind
of litter especially dangerous?

Litter can also be very dirty.
It attracts animals which spread
germs and disease.

Litter harms wildlife

The rubbish we leave lying around may kill or hurt the animals and birds that discover it.

Empty cans and bottles are traps for tiny shrews and mice.   They crawl inside, then can't get out – ever.

27

28

Bin it!

We are all responsible for our own rubbish.   Bin it!   This is the best way to protect wildlife and stop litter.

In what kind of places do you think there should be plenty of bins?

Do you think it is a good idea to make bins attractive?

Index